FAIRIES AND ELVES

Shannon Knudsen

Lerner Publications Company · Minneapolis

Lerner Publications Company
A division of Lerner Publishing Group, Inc.
241 First Avenue North
Minneapolis, MN 55401 U.S.A.

Website address: www.lernerbooks.com

Library of Congress Cataloging-in-Publication Data

Knudsen, Shannon, 1971–
    Fairies and elves / by Shannon Knudsen.
        p.   cm.   — (Fantasy chronicles)
    Includes bibliographical references and index.
    ISBN 978–0–8225–9979–1 (lib. bdg. : alk. paper)
    1. Fairies—Juvenile literature. 2. Elves—Juvenile literature. I.Title.
GR549.K655 2010
398.21—dc22   2008050207

Manufactured in the United States of America
1 2 3 4 5 6 – BP – 15 14 13 12 11 10

TABLE OF CONTENTS

CHAPTER 1

THE CHARMS OF FAIRIES

Imagine yourself on vacation at your great-grandmother's house in Scotland. Gran is fun, but she's a bit strange sometimes. She always tells old stories about the Fair Folk who live under the hill behind her house. You love listening to her tales of fairy feasts and charms, but you're sure all that stuff is just a bunch of superstition. You even laughed at her this afternoon when she warned you not to stay out past dark.

Maybe she was right. You left during daytime, but now it's pitch black except for a sliver of moonlight. You're standing on the very hill Gran told you to avoid. You have no idea how you got there. And somebody is laughing at you—somebody you can't see.

Too bad you aren't better prepared. From what Gran has told you, a sharp iron poker would really come in handy right now. Even a four-leaf clover would help.

The laughter rings out again. It doesn't sound friendly. Then you spot an open doorway in the side of the hill and behind it a tunnel.

"Come with us, come with us!" a voice hisses from behind you.

That's when you realize that this is no Tinker Bell you're dealing with.

Is It a Fairy or an Elf?

The first thing you should know about fairies and elves is something you probably already suspect. What you've just read couldn't actually happen—even if you do have a great-grandmother in Scotland. No one has ever proven that fairies or elves are real, though plenty of people have tried.

The second thing you should know is why this book is about both fairies and elves. You probably think of fairies and elves as quite different. But that's not how people used to see them. *A Midsummer Night's Dream*, one of the most famous plays by the great English writer William Shakespeare, is filled with fairies. That is what Shakespeare often called them. But he also called them elves. Did that confuse the audiences who went to see his play back in 1596? Nope. In those times, the words *fairy* and *elf* meant almost the same thing. But some people considered elves a bit smaller than fairies.

Why would two such different words have the same meaning to

In William Shakespeare's play *A Midsummer Night's Dream*, a fairy king becomes angry at a fairy queen. He tricks her into falling in love with a man who has the head of a donkey.

Shakespeare and the people of his time? The word *fairy* comes from the Latin word *fata*, which means "the Fates." The Fates were three goddesses of Roman and Greek mythology. According to legend, they determined the fate of every person. *Fairy* has been part of the written English language since the 1300s. Historians believe that well before then, in ancient times, people in the British Isles told stories about fairies. The word was originally used to describe many kinds of magic, magical beings, and the places they lived.

A Fairy by Any Other Name

One of the oldest beliefs about fairies is that they don't like to be talked about. They especially dislike hearing the word *fairy*. Just saying that word could attract the unwanted attention of these mischief-making beings. During the Middle Ages (A.D. 500–1500) and beyond, people rarely mentioned fairies in England, Scotland, and Ireland. When they did, they often used positive names such as Fair Folk, Good Neighbors, and Good Folk. It paid to play it safe, just in case the fairies were listening. Fairies were also called Strangers, Wee Folk, Hidden People, or simply Them. If that's not complicated enough, the word *fairy* can be spelled faery or faerie, or it can be shortened to fae or fay.

During the same period in Germany and Scandinavia, people told stories of a similar sort of being. When people from those areas came to live in the British Isles, that being became known as an elf. Over time, most people in the British Isles began to use *fairy* and *elf* to mean the same thing.

So what was a fairy—or an elf—hundreds of years ago? For starters, fairies and elves could be male or female. And they were supernatural. That means that their existence and abilities couldn't be explained by the laws of nature. They had magical powers, and they knew how to use them. For example, fairies

Fairies around the World

The legends and folktales of many countries and cultures include magical beings that are similar to fairies and elves. But they have different names. In Denmark fairies are called *bergfolk*. In Germany fairylike creatures are called *bockmann*, which are half goat. The Tlingit people of Alaska fear evil fairies known as *kushtaka*. These water spirits take on the shape of an otter to trick people into coming close. Then kushtaka devour their victims. Slavic fairies called *wilis* are the spirits of young women who died before their wedding day. They have the power to dance with a man until he falls over dead! The story of the wilis is told in the French ballet *Giselle*.

were almost always invisible to humans unless they wished to be seen. And if you did see them, you probably wouldn't realize what you were looking at. That's because they had the power to change their appearance by shape-shifting. A fairy sometimes took on the shape of a ball of light, a human being, or even an animal.

There is another important aspect of the fairies and elves of yore. They couldn't be trusted, at least not by people. A fairy might be generous or unkind, helpful or dangerous, depending on its mood. Some fairies would do your housework or bring you gifts. But others might strike your cattle with disease or bewitch you to make you get lost in the woods. Fairies might steal from you too. Or they might simply steal *you*. In other words, they might kidnap you.

A couple of British Isles fairies illustrate how different one could be from another. The gentle Nanny Button-Cap visited children as they fell asleep at night. She made sure they were tucked in snug and warm. Lhiannan-shee wasn't quite so kind, though. She liked to charm young men into falling in love with her. They always died of a broken heart.

Fairies and elves could be tall or short, polite or rude. They might be beautiful, like the Irish fairy queen Omagh. Her golden hair was so long that it touched the ground. Others were ugly, like Yallery Brown, a tiny, shriveled male fairy from England. Fairies generally didn't have wings. Many could fly without wings, while others couldn't fly at all. Some lived alone, while others lived in societies ruled by royalty. In short, there were almost as many stories about the lives and doings of fairies and elves as there were humans to listen to and retell them.

CHAPTER 2

TRICKS AND TREATS

According to the old stories, some fairies were naughty. Others were nice. The nice fairies included some you've probably heard of, like Cinderella's fairy godmother. She first appeared in a version of the story written by Charles

Perrault in 1697. Thanks to the fairy godmother's magic, Cinderella attended a ball at a palace. She wore a beautiful gown and arrived in an elegant coach. But kind fairies usually did much simpler things. They didn't make miracles happen. Instead, they often lived in the houses of people they liked and did small favors for them.

An old tale recorded by the Brothers Grimm in 1812 gives an example of this type of fairy or elf help. In "The Elves and the Shoemaker," an old cobbler did not earn enough money to survive. One night he cut his last piece of leather into pieces to make one final pair of shoes. Then he went to bed. To his surprise, the next morning, the pieces had been sewn together into the finest shoes he had ever seen. The shoemaker sold them for much more money than his own work would have brought. He bought more leather, cut it up, and found four pairs of shoes the next morning!

The shoemaker and his wife watched to see who had been visiting during the night. Their helpers turned out to be a pair of happy elves. Noticing that the poor things had no clothes, the wife made them some. The shoemaker fashioned tiny shoes. The grateful couple left the gifts out the next evening. Delighted with their new outfits, the elves danced away into the night without making any shoes. The elves never returned. But for the rest of their lives, the shoemaker and his wife prospered.

This story combines two pieces of fairy lore. First, if a fairy is forced to become a servant as a result of a spell,

The shoemaker and his wife discover who made the leather into beautiful shoes.

Fairy Tales without Fairies

Why do so many fairy tales have nothing to do with fairies? There are no fairies in "Little Red Riding Hood" or lots of other so-called fairy tales. People who study the history of words think that *fairy* used to apply to magic and enchantment of many kinds. So a fairy tale includes magical spells, objects, places, or creatures.

Many fairy tales are known to us thanks to Jacob and Wilhelm Grimm (*right*). The Brothers Grimm lived in Germany from the late 1700s to the mid-1800s. The Grimms collected their tales from the people who liked to tell these magical stories. The brothers wrote down the tales and published them in books.

charm, or curse, a gift of clothing will set it free. The Brothers Grimm didn't explain whether or not the elves in this story were cursed. But since they left after they got the clothing, that seems like a good guess.

The second bit of fairy lore is that generosity always impresses fairies. Even after the elves stopped making shoes, they continued to bless the shoemaker and his wife with good luck. Suppose you are living in the days of fairy believers. You're hoping to receive the good favor of fairies, but you aren't a poor, kindly shoemaker. What should you do? Well, you can still show your generosity by setting out a present for any fairies who happen to wander through your home during the night. Fairy believers often left out a bowl of fresh water or milk, some bread, and perhaps a hunk of cheese.

Another good strategy is to clean your room or even wash the dishes. The fairies and elves of the past admired neatness. Some even left gifts of money during the night for people who kept a tidy house. What better way to impress the Good Folk than to welcome them with a tasty meal *and* a clean kitchen?

How should you act if you meet a fairy face-to-face? Although fairies could be tricky and sometimes lied, they expect honesty from their human neighbors. If a fairy asks you a question, it's best to tell the truth—politely. And remember the importance of being generous. If you're asked for food, drink, or help, be sure to give it.

If you are among the few human beings who receive favors from a fairy, make sure you keep your good fortune to yourself. Telling people that the Fair Folk have given you a hand is the surest way to make your luck run out. In fact, fairies are so private that they'll take away any gifts you reveal. Your money will vanish, and so will your good luck. And the fairies just might think of you the next time they have nothing to do on a quiet evening.

All in Good Fun

The fairies of yore often became bored. At such times, they played tricks simply to entertain themselves. Fairies liked to laugh at human beings. Their powerful magic, called glamour, gave them plenty of ways to make humans look silly. People who were working outdoors or traveling made perfect targets for fairy pranks. A farmer might be crossing his own field and find himself confused. He knows how to get to his house. He can even see it off in the distance. But no matter how hard he tries, he can't reach it. Only when he hears faint laughter in the shadows does he realize what has happened. He's been pixie-led. The Fair Folk have fooled him with their power to change and conceal the appearance of our surroundings.

What should the poor farmer do? If he knows his fairy lore, he'll be fine. By turning his coat inside out, he can break the effects of the fairies' glamour. Or, if he's lucky enough to find a four-leaf clover, he won't be fooled by their illusions. Otherwise, he'll just have to wander his fields until the fairies get bored and release him. If they ever do, that is.

Another story of fairy foolery comes from Ireland. A man named Con was walking home one night when he saw a group of boys playing soccer. He stopped to watch and began to cheer them on. And before long, he joined the game himself. Imagine his surprise when he awoke fifteen miles from home! He'd been tricked into playing with fairies and had kicked the soccer ball for mile after mile without ever realizing what he was doing.

Anyone who insulted or betrayed a fairy could end up in a world of trouble. With a word or a gesture, fairies could bring disease upon crops or farm animals. They could suck all the nutrients from human food. And they could pixie-lead travelers to their deaths by tricking them into wandering off a cliff or into a dangerous bog. They could even cause fairy stroke. This illness left the victim paralyzed and sometimes unable to speak.

Here is a tale about fairies who wanted revenge. Two English girls worked as servants in a big house. Every night they left a bucket of water out for the fairies to drink. Every morning they found a reward of silver coins. One night the girls forgot to put out the water. The fairies woke them up, demanding their drink. One girl got up, but the other was too tired. She refused to help. The next morning, the first girl found silver coins in the bucket as usual. As for the sleepy-head? She found herself lame in one leg, and she remained that way for seven full years.

Fairies make off with a baby on Christmas Eve.

No big deal, right? As long as you were smart enough to avoid upsetting a fairy, you'd be safe from the worst tricks, wouldn't you? Not so fast. The nastiest fairies of all were the ones who didn't care whether you had insulted them or not. They actually enjoyed hurting people.

In Scotland these evildoers belonged to the Unseelie Court. Gentler Scottish fairies belonged to the Seelie Court. Unseelie fairies liked to ride the skies during the night. For fun they picked up

People once believed that bad fairies flew in the skies above the Scottish countryside.

innocent travelers and carried them through the air. The Unseelie fairies often forced their passengers to fire flint arrowheads, called elf-shot, at people and animals on the ground below. Someone hit with elf-shot became sick and sometimes died.

The best protection against attacks by evil fairies was cold iron. A knife or a cross made of this metal was said to ward off or even injure fairies. Sometimes a Bible helped scare away the less friendly of the Good Neighbors too. Still, the safest thing to do was to come home early and stay indoors all night long.

Whether funny or frightening, most fairy tricks started and ended in the human world. Fairies and elves liked their privacy, after all. But every once in a while, they brought humans home to Fairyland to visit—whether the humans liked the idea or not.

People used crosses to scare off evil fairies.

→ CHAPTER 3 ←

AWAY TO FAIRYLAND

Why would fairies and elves want the company of people? According to many old stories from Britain and Ireland, fairies sometimes needed human help in Fairyland. The needest fairies were pregnant mothers. Giving birth could cause terrible danger and pain for fairies, just as it could for human women. But according to folktales, fairies didn't understand childbirth as well as humans did. And they had no midwives—women who were experts at helping mothers give birth safely.

That's why a midwife might answer a nighttime knock at her door to find a tall, noble-looking gentleman she'd never seen before. He begs for her help. Then he carries her on a mighty stallion to a beautiful palace. There she finds the man's wife on a bed of fine linens, about to have a baby. After the midwife helps the mother deliver a healthy child, the man takes her home again. He pays for her kindness with treasure.

The fairy husband in this type of tale has used glamour to disguise himself as a human gentleman and trick the midwife into coming to Fairyland. So how does the midwife realize that she's been among fairies?

In one version of the story, the fairy husband tells the midwife to cover the newborn child with a strange ointment. As she does so, she feels an itch in her eye and rubs it, getting ointment into the eye. Suddenly she sees that the infant, the mother, and the father are not human at all. They're shriveled, nasty-looking creatures. The palace is a cold, damp cave. And the mother's soft bed is just a slimy rock.

The midwife realizes that she's been deceived. The goop she rubbed on the baby is enchanted. It gives the user fairy sight—the ability to see through glamour. The fairy parents want their baby to be able to see through their magic.

Fairies lure a farmer's wife away from her home. What plans do they have for her?

In another version of the story, the midwife learns from a human prisoner that she's among fairies. People believed that fairies captured new human mothers to nurse fairy children. And the fairies lured musicians, singers, and storytellers into Fairyland to provide entertainment. Once in a while, a fairy would fall in love with a human, kidnap that person, and hold a wedding in Fairyland. Any of these unfortunate human captives might warn the midwife of her hosts' true identity. Without such a warning, the midwife might make the terrible mistake of eating or drinking fairy food. The human who did so would be trapped among the Strangers forever.

Enchanted Snacks

A fairy banquet would have looked scrumptious to any human, especially one who had been stuck in Fairyland for days without food. Who could resist platters heaped with flavorful roasted meats, goblets of nectar to drink, and sugary cakes for dessert? Alas, all these tempting treats were fake. Fairies mainly ate weeds and plant stems. They dressed up their food with glamour to appeal to their human guests.

Raised by Fairies

Many fairies and elves wanted human children. Their own offspring were sometimes sickly, and young humans tended to be stronger. Thanks to glamour, fairies found it easy to raise a human child as their own—once they got hold of one, that is.

The easiest way to do that was to simply invite a wandering child to visit. That's what happened to a lad named Robin Jones

A child marvels at a ring of fairies and elves.

who lived in Wales centuries ago. As the story goes, Robin went walking far from home one night. He ventured into a grassy circle, which soon filled with dancing fairies. When they invited Robin to follow them into Fairyland, he couldn't resist.

Down underground they all went. Robin found himself in the loveliest place he could imagine. It was full of birds and flowers in splendid colors. Soon, though, he felt homesick. The fairies agreeably took him back aboveground to his home.

Robin's house looked the same as always, but it was full of

people he didn't recognize. His parents were nowhere to be found. He hurried to a neighbor's house, only to find strangers there as well. These folks remembered hearing about a boy named Robin who had vanished from the fairy circle nearby. But that had happened over a hundred years ago!

In this way, poor Robin Jones discovered one of the most peculiar aspects of Fairyland. Time acted very strangely there, at least from a human's point of view. A few hours in Fairyland might actually be decades in the human world. Visitors or captives had to get out of Fairyland immediately. Otherwise, by the time they reached home, all their loved ones would have died!

Fairyland

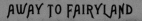

AWAY TO FAIRYLAND

Fairies sometimes added human children to their families by stealing them. This method worked best with babies. Fairies snatched them from their cradles while their parents worked or slept. To trick the parents, the fairies left a false child in place of the real one.

A changeling is discovered in the baby's bed near the fireplace.

These false children were called changelings. There were three types. One was just a lump of wood. The fairies used glamour to make it look like a baby. It would appear to the parents to get sicker and sicker until it died. Another type of changeling was a very old, tired fairy who wanted to be cuddled and fed by loving parents. The old fairy used a glamour disguise to look like the human baby it replaced. Finally, some changelings were real fairy children, again disguised as humans. These children had been rejected by their fairy parents for being too sickly or too difficult to keep.

As you might imagine, none of these false children made for a very happy family in the human world! In fact, some scholars who study fairy folklore have an interesting idea about changelings. They believe that people told changeling stories in many parts of the world as a way of explaining their troubles with their babies. A very cranky child, an ill one, or one who suddenly died could be labeled a changeling. Medical science hadn't yet advanced enough to help people understand much about disease. So the idea that fairies stole healthy, happy children and replaced them with sick ones made sense to many people. It may have been a small comfort after a child's death to picture the "real" baby growing up among the fairies, blessed with good luck forever.

Warding off Danger

Parents in Britain and Ireland tried to protect their children from being kidnapped by fairies. Some fairies hated the color red, so anxious moms pinned a piece of red flannel to their kids' pajamas. Because iron warded off fairies, parents hung a pair of scissors above many cradles. Sometimes they hung the scissors open to make the shape of a cross, for extra security. Or they placed a chain of daisies around a child's neck to keep fairies away.

CHAPTER 4

THE INCREDIBLE SHRINKING FAIRY

A funny thing happened to fairies and elves during the late 1800s. The stories that people had told and believed in for hundreds of years no longer seemed true to most folks. Science and technology had changed the way they lived and viewed the world. Before, for example, parents might have blamed a child's sickness on fairy magic. But in this new era, they were more likely to listen to a doctor's medical explanation. Over time, many people became less willing to believe in beings they couldn't see or touch.

Storytellers didn't forget about fairies and elves, but the stories about them changed. The purpose of the stories was to entertain the listeners rather than to warn them about danger or explain strange events. Fairies themselves became less nasty and a whole lot less scary. The helpful household fairies and elves of old folklore lived on. They still did favors for people and sometimes made a bit of mischief. But a new kind of fairy began to appear in stories and books.

© Disney Enterprises, Inc.

Tinker Bell, from Walt Disney's movie *Peter Pan*

This new fairy was a teeny-tiny female with wings and a pretty, sparkly dress. Did she lure travelers off dark roads as a joke or kidnap babies? Not at all. She was much more likely to be in charge of cleaning flower petals or sprinkling fairy dust on her friends. She might play a little prank now and then. But most of the time, she was as sweet and as cute as she could be.

The most famous representative of these not-so-scary fairies is Tinker Bell. In fact, she may be the most famous fairy of all time. Most of us know Tink as a Disney cartoon. But she began her life as a character in a play by J. M. Barrie called *Peter Pan*, which was published in 1904. A few years later, Barrie made the story of Tinker Bell's adventures with Peter Pan and Wendy into a children's book, *Peter Pan and Wendy*. Tink is so small that when she flies, she looks like a tiny moving light. She has a crush on Peter. And when she feels jealous of his human friend Wendy, she makes mischief. But much of the time she's helpful.

Tinker Bell turned into the fairy we know in 1953. That's when The Walt Disney Company made Barrie's book into an animated movie called *Peter Pan*. Since then she has appeared in many cartoons and has sprinkled fairy dust on the credits of countless Disney films. In 2005 she became the star of the Disney Fairies. It's an entire world of cute fairies, complete with their own books and movies.

During the early years of Tink's life, another friendly fairy came on the scene. A play called *The Tooth Fairy* by Esther Watkins Arnold introduced children to a fairy who brings them money in exchange for lost teeth. The 1927 play launched a long career for the tiny, winged tooth fairy. Parents like to leave money under a child's pillow as evidence that the tooth

The tooth fairy takes a tooth during the night.

THE INCREDIBLE
SHRINKING FAIRY

fairy has visited. It's a popular way to help little kids celebrate the loss of their baby teeth.

If you're not a fan of cutesy-pie fairies, take heart. Some naughty tricksters still play major parts in modern books and movies. The sweet fairy godmother of Charles Perrault's *Cinderella* was her same old self in Walt Disney's animated movie of 1950. But when *Shrek 2* came out in 2004, Fairy Godmother morphed into one mean lady. She pretends to be charming and wise. But she's actually a lying, cheating villain who wants money, power, and more power. She uses her magic in ways that would have made the fairies of the Scottish Unseelie Court proud.

In Walt Disney's *Cinderella*, the Fairy Godmother magically changes Cinderella's dreary dress into a sparkling ball gown.

FAIRIES AND ELVES

The Cottingley Fairies

Two girls from Cottingley, England, discovered during the 1920s just how strongly some people still believed in fairies. The girls took photographs of each other playing in the woods with tiny winged figures. Many adults believed the photos were fake. But a few argued that the photos proved that fairies were real. One of the girls' biggest supporters was Arthur Conan Doyle, the creator of the famous Sherlock Holmes detective stories. Doyle wrote an entire book in support of the Cottingley fairies, called *The Coming of the Fairies*. Decades later, the girls admitted that they had made their woodsy companions out of paper and pins. Talk about a prank that would make a fairy proud!

April-Fooling Fairy

In 2007 a man named Dan Baines created a website with photographs of what he claimed was a mummified fairy found in Derbyshire, England. (Land and weather conditions sometimes mummify, or preserve, a body naturally.) A few days later, Baines admitted that the fairy mummy was a fake. He had made it as an April Fool's Day joke. Still, many people kept insisting that the fairy was real. One person even e-mailed Baines with advice to return the fairy to its gravesite!

Another tribute to scary fairies is *The Spiderwick Chronicles*. This book series has been made into both a movie and a video game. Authors Holly Black and Tony DiTerlizzi think of fairies as an assortment of creepy magical beings. Their books take place in a world of "faeries" that includes brownies, boggarts, sprites, goblins, and elves. The Grace children must learn the ways of the various faeries and conquer many dangers to save themselves and their uncle.

In the *Artemis Fowl* books, author Eoin Colfer also uses the word *fairy* to describe many kinds of creatures that use magic. They include pixies, elves, sprites, and demons. Known as the People, these fairies live underground in the Lower Elements. Artemis, a human boy and criminal mastermind, discovers the existence of the People. In the first book of the series, he plots to steal their gold. As a result, he becomes involved with them in ways he'd never imagined.

Whether good or evil, most modern fairies aren't the powerful enchanters they used to be. Neither are most elves. But *elf* is not always just another name for a fairy. Plenty of elves have their own unique identity. And it isn't a bit like Tinker Bell's.

CHAPTER 5

ENTERTAINING ELVES

By the twentieth century, people began thinking of elves as a particular kind of creature that was different from a fairy. The writer who deserves the most credit for changing the way people thought of elves is surely J. R. R. Tolkien. Tolkien wrote *The Hobbit* and *The Lord of the Rings* in the mid-1900s. This was decades before the publication of the Harry Potter books, *The Spiderwick Chronicles*, and *Artemis Fowl*. Tolkien's stories take place in the imagined world of Middle-earth. It is home to orcs, dwarves, hobbits, elves, and wizards, in addition to humans. Tolkien invented every aspect of his world. He gave it its own geography, history, and even languages.

The elves of Tolkien's books are beautiful, elegant, and tall, like the members of the Seelie Court of Scottish legends. They live for thousands of years, but they never look much older than a human adult. Their powers vary, but they are always intelligent and gifted in the arts. Some, such as Legolas the archer, perform wonderfully in battle. Others, such as the half elf Elrond, Lord of Rivendell, are strong leaders.

The Lord of the Rings, often called *LOTR* for short, was published as three separate books between 1954 and 1955. (There was a paper shortage at the time, and it was far too long to be sold as one book!) For more than fifty years since then, *LOTR* has been a favorite of millions of devoted readers. Tolkien's work has also sparked the imagination of many other writers. He wasn't the first person to write stories about elves and monsters. But he made fantasy

Legolas, played by Orlando Bloom in *The Lord of the Rings* movies, was a fierce warrior.

Santa's Little Helpers

Christmas stories and songs about Santa Claus often mention his short workshop assistants, who build the toys that Santa takes to children on Christmas Eve. Dressed in green, these North Pole elves are known for their cleverness and craftsmanship. We don't know for sure which storyteller invented Santa's elves. They became part of Christmas lore during the 1870s. That's when they started to appear in magazine illustrations and Christmas plays.

books far more popular than they had ever been before. Director Peter Jackson turned the story into three movies during the early 2000s. As a result, Legolas, Galadriel, and the other inhabitants of Middle-earth met a brand-new audience of eager fans.

Elf Entertainment

Tolkien's elves and his other characters changed the way people have fun. The first popular elf-related game was *Dungeons & Dragons*. First published in 1974, *D&D* is a role-playing game. One person creates a world of adventure, while the others play characters within that world. The characters can be any of several races, including elves. *D&D* players imagine they are archer elves or spell casters like those in Tolkien's books. Millions of people have enjoyed the game since the 1970s, and it remains a favorite of Tolkien fans.

Dungeons & Dragons is played with paper and dice. But it has helped game designers bring elves into the digital age. Some of the earliest computer games featured elves, including a 1980 game called *Rogue*. Massively multiplayer online role-playing games (MMORPGs) such as *EverQuest* and *World of Warcraft* allow participants to play as elves too. Each game has its own elf lore. But the idea of pretending to be an elf (or a dwarf or a halfling) goes all the way back to *D&D*.

Players at a convention in Germany all play *World of Warcraft*. Some even take on the role of elves in the online game.

Many video games have been made using the stories and creatures of *The Lord of the Rings*. Then, in 2007, an MMORPG arrived that was set in Middle-earth. It's called *Lord of the Rings Online: Shadows of Angmar.* Players can create a Middle-earth elf and experience adventures that Legolas himself would be proud to share.

J. R. R. Tolkien's elegant elves have taken center stage in modern times. But the short, hardworking fellows of the Brothers Grimm tale "The Elves and the Shoemaker" have not disappeared. Author J. K. Rowling created her own unique version of these tiny workers in her best-selling Harry Potter series. In Harry's world, wizard families keep house-elves as servants. Short, pointy-eared, and highly intelligent, house-elves are gifted with powerful magic. They can travel instantly from one place to another, for example.

Many of Rowling's house-elves are proud to serve their masters. But if a house-elf wants his freedom, he needs the master's cooperation. The master must give the elf a piece of real clothing to replace the pillowcase or towel it normally wears. Rowling's novels connect clothing with freedom, just as in "The Elves and the Shoemaker." In this way, Rowling links her story with those that came before it.

Elves and fairies have been with us for centuries, from the tales of ancient storytellers to J. K. Rowling's novels. We're fascinated by these creatures' magic, cleverness, and mysterious ways. We want their favor and good luck. But we're also scared of the evil they may work upon us. Even though very few of us really believe in elves or fairies anymore, we can't seem to stop making up stories about them. They still work their powerful charm on us.

Selected Bibliography

Ashliman, D. L. *Fairy Lore: A Handbook.* Westport, CT: Greenwood Press, 2006.

BBC. "Fairy Fool Sparks Huge Response." *BBC News.* n.d. http://news.bbc.co.uk/2/hi/uk_news/england/derbyshire/6514283.stm (August 23, 2008).

Briggs, Katherine M. *An Encyclopedia of Fairies: Hobgoblins, Brownies, Bogeys, and Other Supernatural Creatures.* New York: Pantheon Books, 1976.

_____. *The Vanishing People: A Study of Traditional Fairy Beliefs.* London: B. T. Batsford, 1978.

Doyle, Arthur Conan. *The Coming of the Fairies.* 1922. Reprint, London: Pavilion Books, 1997.

Franklin, Anna. *The Illustrated Encyclopedia of Fairies.* New York: Sterling, 2005.

Garry, Jane, and Hasan El-Shamy, eds. *Archetypes and Motifs in Folklore and Literature.* Armonk, NY: M. E. Sharpe, 2005.

IGN Entertainment. "Magic and Memories: The Complete History of Dungeons & Dragons." *GameSpy.* N.d. http://pc.gamespy.com/articles/538/538262p3.html (September 26, 2008).

Keightley, Thomas. *The Fairy Mythology.* 1850. Reprint, New York: Haskell House, 1968.

Narváez, Peter, ed. *The Good People: New Fairylore Essays.* New York: Garland Publishing, 1991.

Purkiss, Diane. *Troublesome Things: A History of Fairies and Fairy Stories.* New York: Penguin Putnam, 2000.

Restad, Penne L. *Christmas in America: A History.* New York: Oxford University Press, 1995.

Shakespeare, William. *A Midsummer Night's Dream. The Complete Works of William Shakespeare.* N.d. http://shakespeare.mit.edu/midsummer/full.html (August 24, 2008).

Tolkien, J. R. R. *The Lord of the Rings.* Boston: Houghton Mifflin, 2005.

Further Reading and Websites
Books

Black, Holly, and Tony DiTerlizzi. *The Spiderwick Chronicles: The Field Guide.* New York: Simon & Schuster, 2003. The first book in the five-volume *Spiderwick Chronicles* introduces nine-year-old twin brothers Jared and Simon Grace, as well as their thirteen-year-old sister, Mallory. The Graces move into a spooky old home, Spiderwick Estate, which once belonged to their uncle. There the kids discover a hidden library and a mysterious book that claims to be a field guide to "faeries." The book is by their uncle—who is missing.

Colfer, Eoin. *Artemis Fowl.* New York: Viking Press, 2001. If you were a teenage criminal mastermind with time on your hands, what would you do? For Artemis Fowl, the answer is simple: steal the fairies' gold. Another first book in a long and successful series, *Artemis Fowl* presents a world in which fairies of many kinds live in hiding underground. Artemis discovers their existence and plots to steal their fortune, but he finds that getting away with this crime won't be as easy as he'd hoped.

Reinhart, Matthew, and Robert Sabuda. *Encyclopedia Mythologica: Fairies and Magical Creatures.* Somerville, MA: Candlewick Press, 2008. A three-dimensional look at the darker side of fairy lore, this book combines pop-up illustrations with facts about the tricks and talents of fairies and fairylike beings from all over the world. Enchanted animals such as the unicorn and Pegasus get their share of the attention too.

Rowling, J. K. *Harry Potter and the Chamber of Secrets.* New York: Arthur A. Levine Books, 1999. The second volume in the worldwide best-selling Harry Potter series introduces a house-elf named Dobby. Dobby is bound to serve the nasty Draco Malfoy, an enemy of Harry's. Unlike most house-elves, Dobby hates his fate. But his good heart and desire to help Harry change his life for the better.

Websites

Hidden Ireland: A Guide to Irish Fairies
http://www.irelandseye.com/animation/intro.html
This site offers an illustrated field guide to several magical beings of Ireland. Viewers can learn about changelings, leprechauns, and the banshee, a spirit who wails in grief when someone from a famous

family is about to die. Visitors can also send a fairy e-card and listen to traditional Irish music.

The UnMuseum: The Case of the Cottingley Fairies
http://www.unmuseum.org/fairies.htm
The UnMuseum examines what it calls "unnatural mysteries" of many kinds. Here readers can learn about the Cottingley fairies and the two girls who created them. Two of the fake photographs that the girls created are shown. The site also describes how the truth about the fraud was finally revealed, more than seventy years after it began!

Movies and TV

Elf. DVD. New York: New Line Home Entertainment, 2004. Will Ferrell, Bob Newhart, and Mary Steenburgen star in this Christmas comedy. Ferrell plays Buddy, one of Santa's toy shop workers. Buddy has lived all his life at the North Pole, but he isn't quite like the other elves. He's much too big, and he's terrible at making toys. Eventually he discovers that he's actually a human who was adopted as a baby by Santa's helpers. Buddy travels to New York City to track down his real father, a nasty guy who has plenty to learn about the meaning of Christmas.

The Fairly OddParents. Season 6, Vol. 1. DVD. Burbank, CA: Nicktoons Productions, 2008. Daran Norris stars as ten-year-old Timmy in this animated TV comedy. Timmy has an unusual family. Instead of just a typical mom and dad, he has two fairy godparents, Wanda and Cosmo. These "fairly odd parents" mean to help, just like the kind fairies of the old stories. But they often cause silly and unexpected troubles with their magic wands.

The Lord of the Rings. DVD. New York: New Line Home Entertainment, 2001 to 2003. Viggo Morensen and Elijah Wood star in this movie trilogy directed by Peter Jackson. The trilogy brings J. R. R. Tolkien's masterpiece to the screen in three parts based on the three volumes in which the book was first published (1954 to 1955). *The Fellowship of the Ring* introduces Frodo Baggins and his mission to destroy the One Ring before the evil Sauron claims it. *The Two Towers* builds on the suspense as the Fellowship encounters devastating setbacks in their effort to complete their quest. Finally, *The Return of the King* concludes the story with an epic battle. Several elf characters, including Legolas, Galadriel, and Arwen, play important roles in these films.

Shrek 2. DVD. Burbank, CA: DreamWorks Animated Productions, 2004. The very nasty Fairy Godmother causes lots of trouble for Shrek and Princess Fiona. Shrek, played by Mike Myers, and Fiona, played by Cameron Diaz, are traveling to meet Fiona's parents in Far Far Away. The Fairy Godmother uses her magic and every trick she can think of to try to get Fiona to marry her son, Prince Charming, so that Charming will become king. Luckily, her magic wand ends up between the teeth of Donkey just when Fairy Godmother needs it the most!

Index

About the Author

Shannon Knudsen has written thirty books for kids on subjects ranging from orangutans to the life of Thomas Edison. She lives in Tucson, Arizona, with a cat, a dog, and several kinds of cactuses.

Photo Acknowledgments

The images in this book are used with the permission of: © John Anster Fitzgerald/The Bridgeman Art Library/Getty Images, pp. 1, 23; © Mary Evans Picture Library/Alamy, pp. 6, 15, 22, 26; © Lebrecht Music and Arts Photo Library/Alamy, pp. 12, 24; © SuperStock, Inc./SuperStock, p. 13; © Sir Joseph Noel Paton/The Bridgeman Art Library/Getty Images, p. 17; © Travelpix Ltd/Photographer's Choice/Getty Images, p. 18; © Barry David Marcus/SuperStock, p. 19; © Victoria & Albert Museum, London/Art Resource, NY, p. 25; © Disney Enterprises, Inc., pp. 30, 32; © iStockphoto.com/Heather Laing, p. 31; © Fortean Picture Library, p. 33 (both); Dan Baines/Rex Features USA, p. 34; THE LORD OF THE RINGS: THE TWO TOWERS © New Line Productions, Inc. ™ The Saul Zaentz Company d/b/a Tolkien Enterprises under license to New Line Productions, Inc. All Rights Reserved. Still courtesy of P. Vinet/New Line Cinema/ZUMA Press, p. 38; © Waltraud Grubitzsch/epa/CORBIS, p. 40.

Illustrations © Bill Hauser/Independent Picture Service, pp. 4–5, 10, 20–21, 28, 36–37. All page backgrounds illustrated by © Bill Hauser/Independent Picture Service.

Front Cover: © Kerem Beyit; © iStockphoto.com/Michelle Bennett (background).